Simple Rules for Effective Business Communication

Jennifer Mosher

This is an IndieMosh book
brought to you by MoshPit Publishing
an imprint of Mosher's Business Support Pty Ltd

PO Box 147
Hazelbrook NSW 2779

indiemosh.com.au

Copyright © Jennifer Mosher 2018

The moral right of the author has been asserted in accordance with the Copyright Amendment (Moral Rights) Act 2000.

All rights reserved. Except as permitted under the Australian Copyright Act 1968 (for example, fair dealing for the purposes of study, research, criticism or review) no part of this publication may be reproduced, stored in a retrieval system, or transmitted in any form or by any means, electronic, mechanical, photocopying, recording or otherwise, without the written permission of the publisher.

Cataloguing-in-Publication entry is available from the National Library of Australia:
http://catalogue.nla.gov.au/

Title:	Simple Rules for Effective Business Communication
Author:	Mosher, Jennifer (1961–)
ISBNs:	978-1-925739-77-0 (paperback)
	978-0-987173-11-9 (ebook – epub)
	978-0-987564-00-9 (ebook – mobi)

Cover design and layout by Ally Mosher at allymosher.com

***Who Caught the Yawn?*
and
*Where Did the Sneeze Go?***

– a two-in-one paperback for children,
also available as individual ebooks and
audiobooks.

Illustrated by Todd Sharp, these titles
explore the daily and weekly life
of young Max.

Find out more at:

jennifermosher.com.au

Contents

Introduction 1

Rule 1: Start with the end in mind 5

Rule 2: Your communications are a tool for promoting your business 6

Rule 3: Know your limitations 8

Rule 4: KISS: Keep It Simple, Stupid! 9

Rule 5: Know your audience 10

Rule 6: The nitty gritty 11

Rule 7: Learn from others 12

Rule 8: Consider the language appropriate for your communication 13

Rule 9: Consider the emotions in your communication 15

Rule 10: Observe the basic outline of most communications 17

Ten simple steps for your next communication 19

Thank you for reading 21

About the author 22

Introduction

To be able to implement some simple rules for effective business communication, there are some basics which must first be considered, and which can be identified using the 'What, Where, When, Why and How' type of question.

The first thing to be comfortable with is a definition of what communication actually is.

Question: What *is* communication?

Answer: Getting the message across. Not just sending it but sending it in such a way that the receiver understands what you're sending.

You can send out a message in Morse Code, or give a speech in Italian, but if your audience doesn't understand Morse Code or Italian, then are you really communicating?

You can answer a question sarcastically, but if your audience doesn't see your facial expression or hear it in your voice, will they understand what you're really saying? So more than just the words and the language, it's about the meaning. It's about *getting the message across*.

Question: Why do we communicate?

Answer: To get a result that we want. Quite simply, it's a form of manipulation.

From the moment we are born, we use communication to get what we want: a baby cries to indicate that it needs food, a nappy change, or simply just a little comforting.

Every communication we make is a form of manipulation, but not necessarily the bad kind. While it can be as simple as a warm smile to make someone feel better, every communication we make is an attempt in some way to get someone else to think or do something that we want them to do.

Question: When and how do we communicate in business?

Answer: As well as with every letter, email or telephone call, we communicate every time we open our mouths, put on our uniforms, drive our branded cars, roll our eyes or lean forward in conversation – every miniscule item of our behaviour is a form of communication.

A roll of the eyes when uttering something sarcastic communicates that the words are not to be taken literally.

Navy drill trousers, a blue shirt with insignia and a radio communicate someone in authority – a police officer, transit police, etc., while a white lab coat communicates someone working in a medical or scientific field. These clothes may not be an accurate communication, but due to their historical use, that's the first impressions they will give until we gather more information.

The language we use communicates our level or lack of education, and our level or lack of respect for our audience.

The way we drive or park our branded car communicates our respect for our community and the law, or lack of thereof!

In the twenty-first century, business communication takes many forms:

- telephone calls, SMS or texts
- face to face, in person

- face to face, via technology – Skype, webcam
- emails, letters, reports
- marketing materials – brochures, newsletters, websites
- social networking – Facebook, Twitter, LinkedIn, YouTube videos
- presentations, stalls, marketing activities
- products and services
- branding on uniforms, vehicles, in the workplace
- general appearance – ours and our workplace's.

Rule 1: Start with the end in mind

What are you trying to achieve?

What do you want to have happen as a result of your communication? Do you want your audience to actually *do* something, or are you just hoping to inform? This is an important consideration when preparing your marketing materials. Are you hoping people will buy, or are you just aiming to increase brand awareness?

If you're hoping to get someone to do something, consider the possible outcomes of that person actually responding to your communication in the way you hope. Is it likely that what you *think* you want will bring a whole new set of problems, or make matters worse, rather than better?

Think through the possible consequences, particularly when creating communication in conflict.

Rule 2:
Your communications are a tool for promoting your business

Use your logo, your colours, your fonts, your 'business personality' – in other words, use your 'brand'.

Maintain a standard.

Get your staff to adopt your standard.

Decide how you want people to view your business:

- honest
- great for bargains
- high end
- innovative etc.

This is where driving that branded car within the speed limits communicates that your business respects the law and the other users on the road. And the same goes for leaving it in the disabled parking spot while you pop in for a loaf of bread. Dropping litter while wearing your logo shirt or uniform will attract the wrong sort of attention on social media.

Be careful what you're communicating about your business whenever the public may see, hear or even smell you!

Rule 3:
Know your limitations

Clint Eastwood's best-loved character, Dirty Harry, once famously uttered, 'A man's got to know his limitations.' It's great advice.

If you don't know how to build a sentence using five syllable words, then don't!

If you don't know the meaning of a word, don't use it. Use something you understand.

If your spelling, punctuation and grammar aren't the best, get someone else to polish your work up before going to print or before you give that speech. If you don't have someone in-house who can do this efficiently for you, then engage an editor, especially if getting it wrong could lose you a contract, a client or a court case!

Rule 4:
KISS:
Keep It Simple, Stupid!

Don't digress or sidetrack your audience.

Don't try to build really long, convoluted sentences or concepts – keep it logical and shorten the sentences. One or two concepts per sentence is more than enough.

If there's no prerequisite for lots of five syllable words, then keep it to two, three and four syllable ones!

'Avoiding clichés like the plague' is one thing, but avoiding jargon is probably even more important.

Rule 5:
Know your audience

If it's likely your audience won't understand a particular word, sentence or concept you plan to use, then simplify. Use smaller, more direct words, or shorter sentences.

Avoid industry-specific jargon unless communicating specifically to your industry.

Think about what you want your audience to do as a result of your communication, and then try to work out what you would need to say to get them to do that willingly.

Get inside their heads! What is their education? Their socio-economic or age demographic? What are their expectations? Their morals? What do you have to do to manipulate them into seeing it your way? Who is in your audience?

- Staff?
- Clients?
- Prospects?
- Other businesses or affiliates?
- Government or other authorities?

Rule 6:
The nitty gritty

For written communication, use your spell checker. Your spell checker won't catch everything, but at least it's a good start.

Get someone else to check your written work, preferably someone with better language skills and knowledge. A sign saying 'Apologies for any Incontinence' will not be picked up by your spell checker. (And yes, this did happen! These signs were posted all over the doors at the local high school auditorium.)

If in doubt, send it out to a professional to check. Editors and proofreaders can be found across the internet. Rates across the industry vary from $30 to more than $100 per hour, and you will often get what you pay for. Search for 'professional editors [country]' to find one suited to your needs. For example, if you're an Australian who's written a novel in US English, you should consider using an American editor. In Australia, for writing in Australian English, try iped-editors.org

Rule 7:
Learn from others

If you see or hear an example of what you feel is good communication, remember it for future use.

Likewise, if you notice an example of what you feel is bad communication, remember that – then steer clear of it! And this lesson applies to pretty much everything in life. It's one thing to emulate people we admire, but also good policy to make sure we don't make the same mistakes we see others making.

Rule 8: Consider the language appropriate for your communication

- Formal
- Plain English
- Conversational
- Text/SMS/Gangsta/Colloquial and Slang

These days, Plain English is the Australian government recommended standard for everyday commercial use.

Formal language is now generally reserved for legal documents, and even these days many legal documents are being rewritten in Plain English so that they are more accessible to more people.

If you're creating a business document, whether a letter, email or marketing material, a mix of Plain English and Conversational should cover your needs. You can still be polite and efficient if required, but you don't need to resort to long-winded sentences with rarely-used words.

If you're communicating with your audience using social media, be careful to avoid offensive language and ideas, and don't use text abbreviations such as 'wtf' unless they're normally used by your specific audience.

And if you only understand the *sentiment* of 'wtf' and not the words it stands for, then you definitely shouldn't use it!!

Rule 9:
Consider the emotions in your communication

When you communicate, it's important to not just consider your emotions, but also the emotions you're trying to stir in the recipient.

Think about what you want the recipient to do. Why are you communicating about this issue? Is it a communication so that you feel better? Or so that the recipient feels better? Or worse?

If you're angry, think about your motivation. *Why* are you angry? Is it possible that you're angry with yourself? Did you bring about the situation by not being clear enough, or by delivering a service or product that wasn't quite up to standard?

Look in the mirror: are you sure none of the blame is yours?

If you're happy that the recipient needs to hear what you have to say, consider the following:

- Can you afford to ruin this relationship?
- Do you want to free yourself from this relationship?
- Would you prefer that the relationship continue?

Be careful what you choose!

If it's not an anger-related issue, are you communicating for the recipient's benefit, or for your own self-esteem? For example, are you sending a sympathy card to someone you don't know well because you feel for them in their pain? Or are you doing it in the hope that they'll become more aware of you and/or your business?

Don't let your own self-esteem issues creep into your motivation, and don't use other people's personal issues as an opportunity for marketing.

Rule 10:
Observe the basic outline of most communications

a. Beginning or introduction

b. Middle or bulk of information

c. End or wrap up

Every formal communication, including phone calls, should somehow have a Beginning, a Middle and an End. The only person excused from this is Quentin Tarantino.

Plan your communication logically, particularly your phone calls. Business people don't have time to hear you waffle around while you work your way up to why you're calling. Get to the point quickly.

And before dialling, consider: *What will I say if I have to leave a message?* Work your most important sentences out first, then dial.

If you're having trouble, make dot points, get them in order, delete the unnecessary ones, then flesh out what's left – particularly if it's a written communication.

    Add an introduction and a wrap up and, hopefully, voila!

Ten simple steps for your next communication

1. Who are you targeting?
2. What do you want them to do?
3. What emotion do you want to express, if any?
4. What sort of language should you be using?
5. Make notes of the things you wish to express or discuss.
6. Sort your notes into a logical order.
7. Create the body of your communication by padding out the notes into sentences and paragraphs.
8. Write your introduction and your wrap-up.
9. Check it – once, twice, three times.
10. Send!

Thank you for reading

If you have learned just one thing from this little book, please log in to where you purchased it and leave a review letting me know what that one thing was.

Happy communicating and thank you for your time!

Jennifer Mosher

About the author

Jennifer is an Australian business owner, self publishing facilitator and former editor.

She is also the founder and owner of:

Mosher's Business Support Pty Ltd
(moshers.com.au)
which is the holding company for:

IndieMosh
(indiemosh.com.au)
the self-publishing facilitation service
for Australian authors

One Thousand Words Plus
(onethousandwordsplus.com)
the international book marketing site

MoshPit Publishing
(moshpitpublishing.com.au)
the publishing imprint for IndieMosh

and ...

narratorINTERNATIONAL
(narratorINTERNATIONAL.com)
the former online creative writing site
which commenced life as
narratorMAGAZINE Blue Mountains

Find out more about Jennifer on her
(occasionally updated and often very
opinionated) blog at:

jennifermosher.com.au

Or follow her on Facebook at:

facebook.com/JenniferMosherAustralia/

www.ingramcontent.com/pod-product-compliance
Lightning Source LLC
LaVergne TN
LVHW020741090526
838202LV00057BA/6165